STEPPARENTS

MUM

STEPDAD

BY HOLLY DUHIG

BookLife
PUBLISHING

©2018
BookLife Publishing
King's Lynn
Norfolk PE30 4LS

A catalogue record for this
book is available from the
British Library.

ISBN: 978-1-78637-290-1

Written by:
Holly Duhig

Edited by:
Kirsty Holmes

Designed by:
Danielle Rippengill

Image Credits

All images are courtesy of Shutterstock.com, unless otherwise specified. With thanks to Getty Images, Thinkstock Photo and iStockphoto. Front Cover – szefei, prapann, Alexander Lysenko, Mc Satori, Kim Reinick, Yellow Cat, nafterphoto, Quang Ho, Madlen. Images used on every spread – Red_Spruce, MG Drachal, Alexander Lysenko, Kues, Flas100, Kanate, Mc Satori, Nikolaeva. 1 – szefei, prapann. 2 – Africa Studio. 4–7 – Africa Studio. 7 – alexmisu. 8 – Africa Studio. 9 – Photographee.eu, Filip Fuxa. 10 – Nopparat Nambunyen. 11 – Monkey Business Images, wavebreakmedia. 12 & 13 – Africa Studio. 14 – Tom Wang. 15 – Africa Studio. 16 – Joshua Resnick, udra11. 17 – Africa Studio. 18 – Brocreative. 19 – Africa Studio. 20 – Natalya Chumak. 21–23 – Africa Studio.

CONTENTS

WORDS THAT LOOK LIKE **THIS** CAN BE FOUND IN THE GLOSSARY ON PAGE 24.

My Family ♡

This is my family. There is me, my mum, my stepdad and my stepbrother.

My name is Ella. My mum's name is Candice.
For a long time, it was just me and her.

JOINING FAMILIES

When I was six, my mum introduced me to Alex and his son, Kurtis. She said she met Alex at her job and they really liked each other.

ALEX

KURTIS

OUR HOUSE

ALEX AND KURTIS CAME TO OUR HOUSE TO PLAY.

After a while, Mum told me that Alex and Kurtis were going to stay over at our house. I was really worried at first. I didn't want to have to share my mum with other people.

Alex and Kurtis didn't move in straight away. At first, they only stayed at our house at the weekends. It wasn't long before I started to look forward to seeing them again!

When they moved in, our spare room became Kurtis's room. It was very plain, so I helped him decorate it. He brought all his toys and games with him.

KURTIS SHARED HIS TOYS WITH ME AND I SHARED MINE WITH HIM.

WEDDINGS

Last year, Mum and Alex decided to get married.
I was a bridesmaid and Kurtis was a **page boy**.

I GOT TO HOLD
A **BOUQUET**.

THE WEDDING CAKE WAS DELICIOUS!

MY STEP-GRANDMA AND STEP-GRANDAD.

Lots of people came to the wedding. I got to meet the rest of Alex and Kurtis's family, including Kurtis's grandparents, who are now my step-grandparents.

Changing Names

MUM CHANGED HER NAME BY SIGNING THE **MARRIAGE REGISTER**.

When people get married, they often change their **surnames**. My mum changed her surname to match Alex's. They are now Mr and Mrs Hughes.

I changed my surname to Hughes too. It made me feel a part of our new family. Now mine and Kurtis's last names match!

MY MUM
IS NOW KURTIS'S
STEPMUM.

Lu Cháng is my best friend at school. She also has a stepdad but she hasn't changed her name. This is because she mostly lives with her **birthparent** and wanted to keep the same surname as him.

My Best Friend, Lu

I never knew my dad. It's always just been me and Mum, so I used to have her surname. When she changed her name, I wanted to change mine too.

It was difficult getting used to having a stepfamily at first.
I didn't like it when Alex told me to tidy my room, and Kurtis
didn't like it when my mum made him do his homework.

I now know that Alex just wants to look after me like a father. Sometimes he asks me to do chores, but other times he takes me to fun things like dance class.

FAMILY FUN

We go on lots of days out as a family. One time we visited the **aquarium**. We saw sharks!

Me and Mum like to go shopping!

Even though Alex and Kurtis live with us, Mum still takes me on days out where it's just the two of us.

New Beginnings

My New Brother or Sister!

The best thing about our family is that it's still growing.
My mum and Alex have decided to have a baby together.

The new baby will be mine and Kurtis' **half-sibling**.
There's been lots to do to get ready for a new baby.
I helped Mum and Alex paint the **nursery**.

Families are always growing and changing.
This can be scary at first but it can also be really exciting!

I love my mum, my stepdad and my stepbrother – and I know
I will love the new baby too. I wouldn't change my family for
the whole world!

Glossary and Index

Glossary

aquarium	a place containing tanks of many different sea creatures
birthparent	biological parent
bouquet	a specially arranged bunch of flowers
half-sibling	a sibling who shares one biological parent
marriage register	a list of all the people who have got married
nursery	a room in a house for a baby or young child
surnames	a last name that is passed down through the family

Index